WHEN IT RAINS

WHEN IT RAINS

ANTHONY BLACK

When it Rains
first published 2014 by
Scirocco Drama
An imprint of J. Gordon Shillingford Publishing Inc.

Scirocco Drama Editor: Glenda MacFarlane
Cover design by Terry Gallagher/Doowah Design Inc.
Cover photo by Mell Hattie
From left to right: Francine Deschepper, Anthony Black, Samantha Wilson, Marc Bendavid
Author photo by Michael De Sadeleer
Printed and bound in Canada on 100% post-consumer recycled paper.

We acknowledge the financial support of the Manitoba Arts Council and The Canada Council for the Arts for our publishing program.

Library and Archives Canada Cataloguing in Publication

Black, Anthony, 1977-, author
When it rains / Anthony Black.

A play.
ISBN 978-1-927922-00-2 (pbk.)

I. Title.

PS8603.L243W44 2014 C812'.6 C2014-901016-8

J. Gordon Shillingford Publishing
P.O. Box 86, RPO Corydon Avenue, Winnipeg, MB Canada R3M 3S3

Acknowledgements

The play was developed with support from the Nova Scotia Department of Tourism, Culture, and Heritage and Playwrights Atlantic Resource Centre.

I would like to thank the following artists who participated in workshops and readings of the script: Jackie Torrens, Garry Williams, Gordon Gammie, Annie Valentina, Andrew Cull, and Jean Morpurgo. Thanks also to Ann-Marie Kerr, Bill Black, Greg Scherkoske, and the members of The Common.

Production Notes

A note on punctuation and pauses, and pronunciations.

I've tried to be precise in the punctuation, but I'm sure there are spots where I don't follow my own rules.

Here's what I intend.

A beat is shorter than a pause.

A slash (/) in the middle of a line indicates an overlap. (ie the next line should begin and the line interrupted should finish. An em dash (—) indicates a line that is cut off cleanly. An ellipse (...) is used when the words stop but the thought continues. Louis is spoken in the French pronunciation. He speaks with a thick French accent.

A Note on the Text

This text is a partial document of the original production of *When it Rains*. The play was written for a very specific production design in which a single projector is used as the only source of light. It is impossible to properly convey in words how the projected elements and animations and how they functioned, as well as how they interacted with the performance. The use of projections has an effect on the rhythm of scenes, as well as their content. For example, there are a number of instances in the script where there is projected text. As important as what the text says is its placement in the visual composition, the rhythm with which it fades in and out, even its font. Similarly, the sound design plays an integral role. I have tried in places to convey how the projection and sound worked but this is incomplete.

The play is divided into three acts but should run straight through with no intermission.

The Voice Over (V.O.) is a computer generated voice (female).

Production History

was originally produced by 2b theatre company and premiered at the Bus Stop Theatre, Halifax, NS, on April 19, 2011 with the following cast:

ALAN:.. Conor Green

ANNA:.. Samantha Wilson

LOUIS: ....Sébastien Labelle

SYBIL:...Francine Deschepper

Directed by Anthony Black

Projection Design by Nick Bottomley

Sound Design and Dramaturgy by Christian Barry

Costume Design by Leesa Hamilton

Production and Stage Management by Louisa Adamson

Assistant Director: Simon Bloom

Scene

A city

Time

Today

Anthony Black

Anthony Black is a versatile artist who works as a writer, director, actor, designer, and as artistic co-director of Canada's internationally acclaimed 2b theatre company. His plays include *When it Rains, Invisible Atom,* and *Homage.* Collaborative creation and writing projects include *The Story of Mr. Wright* (with Christian Barry and Globe Theatre Young company), and *Soul Alone* (with Conor Green).

His plays have been performed at theatres and festivals across Canada and internationally. Anthony is a graduate of York University and the National Theatre School's Directing Program and a member of Playwrights Atlantic Resource Centre. He lives in Halifax with his wife Ann-Marie Kerr and his daughter Sophia.

Prologue

The actors enter and find their places They look at the audience.

V.O.: This is the story of four people.

Music starts and lights fade to black.Then a circle of white light illuminates each actor's head and shoulders. As each character is named, their names appear over their heads.

Alan,

Projection: ALAN

Anna,

Projection: ANNA

Sybil,

Projection: SYBIL

And Louis.

Projection: LOUIS

SYBIL and LOUIS' names and light circles fade down as they turn their heads to look at ALAN and ALAN and ALAN and ANNA turn to look at at other.

Alan and Anna are brother and sister. They are children of a mother who was a judicial clerk and a father who was a murderer, although having never met him and not knowing anything of his crimes, this had no effect on how they grew up or on who they became.

ALAN and ANNA turn to look at the audience for a beat. Then ALAN turns his head to look at SYBIL, whose name and light circle re-establish as ANNA's disappear.

Alan is married to Sybil.

ALAN looks lovingly at SYBIL, who smiles and waves at the audience.

Eight years ago, Sybil accidentally got on the wrong bus and ended up several blocks from her intended destination—an interview with a potential employer in a government agency. Realizing that being late would likely ruin her chances at getting the job, she decided to miss the interview entirely and stopped into a pastry shop. The man behind the counter,

ALAN turns to look at the audience and SYBIL turns to look at ALAN.

Alan, was a graduate student in mathematics, although they did not discuss this at the time.

Alan did not actually work in the pastry shop. In fact he was another customer. He had ordered and eaten an almond croissant before he realized that his wallet was at home. Embarrassed, he volunteered to work off the two dollars and thirty cents he owed the shop, which worked out to approximately twenty minutes at what was then the provincial minimum wage.

And so it was that, through a series of small and unremarkable coincidences, Alan and Sybil met.

ALAN and SYBIL turn to gaze into each other's eyes, smiling.

Two years and seven months later, they were engaged.

A small circle of light illuminates their hands, held, and SYBIL's engagement ring and wedding band.

This is slightly shorter than the average pre-marriage courtship period for North Americans of European descent.

All turn to look at the audience. The V.O. counts in the musical timing, like a dance instructor:

Four five six

The light circles and names of characters all re-establish as the four characters begin to sway in time with the music. After a beat, ALAN and SYBIL's lights and names dim.

Twelve years ago, Anna had participated in a six-week university study-abroad program in France. In her application she claimed that she was able to speak French, though in reality she spoke not a word. On the first day, she met a young philosophy student named Louis.

ANNA and LOUIS turn to look at each other, smiling.

They did not talk much over the next six weeks, choosing instead to express their feelings through a tumultuous sexual discourse.

ANNA and LOUIS' swaying transforms into something a little more sultry for a few bars, as though discovering how well their bodies move together.

At the end of the six weeks, they exchanged addresses. Louis promised to write and Anna promised to learn French, although their respective senses of obligation evaporated almost as soon as Anna boarded the plane home,

They resume the regular swaying and look out to the audience.

the same way that the strongest of summer camp friendships can emerge and disappear without regret or disappointment.

ANNA's light and name fade out. LOUIS' swaying stops.

Over the next decade, Louis went on to complete his undergrad, graduate degree, and then PhD.

LOUIS gives a bit of a nod to the audience before his name and light fade out and ANNA's light and name re-establish. Through the following her swaying gets slower and slower, until she stops.

In the meantime Anna had drifted from job to job, ambition to ambition. With each passing year, she felt herself moving away from the vitality that had characterized her youth. She *felt* less pretty and *was* less thin. One night, while out on the town with friends,

ANNA slowly turns toward LOUIS whose name and light are re-establishing. Their faces convey the slow dawning of rekindled excitement and amazement at the serendipity of it all.

she had a chance reunion with Louis, who, through sheer coincidence, had just taken a job in the philosophy department of a local university.

Their bodies seem to remember the way they moved together and begin the sultry movements from before, building up to an almost orgasmic crescendo over the following.

Meeting Louis again reminded Anna of the things she had once been and now felt she was not.

That night they resumed their passionate sexual discourse where they had left off.

ALAN and SYBIL turn to look at ANNA and LOUIS. The sultriness of their dance has now peaked and the intensity of the movement decresendos.

They got married in what, to those around them, was a surprisingly short amount of time, enjoying for a time, the memory of lust

ANNA and LOUIS look out to the audience,

before the reality of their unhappiness became apparent.

The swaying stops and all four look out at the audience as their names and light circles re-establish.

This is the story of four people.

Music swell as lights fade to black for the transition. Lightning flash and thunder clap into:

Act I

Scene 1

SYBIL and ALAN have just finished dinner. SYBIL is pregnant. They look at each other, smiling and in love.

SYBIL: *(Romantic almost to the point of irony.)* What are the chances?

ALAN: *(Laughs.)* Of what?

SYBIL: That we'd be here?

ALAN: I don't really catch your meaning. Here like at home? I don't know, pretty good I guess.

SYBIL: No, not that. Well, in a way yes, *that*. I don't know, I mean…here we are, we have happiness…

ALAN: Yes.

SYBIL: We're living in one of the wealthiest countries in the world—

ALAN: Yeah but wealth isn't happiness—

SYBIL: No I know that, but we're happy—

ALAN: No, we are.

SYBIL: We both have jobs we like,—

ALAN: Well—

SYBIL: OK, but they could be a lot worse.

ALAN: Yes, no that's true.

SYBIL: *(Putting her hand on her belly.)* And of course we've been blessed.

ALAN: Well "blessed" implies a blesser, but yes I see what you're saying, go on.

Beat.

SYBIL: And really, think about it, that this little coagulation of rock just happens to have water and air, and that life somehow sparked itself into existence, and cells divided, and Neanderthals died off but for some reason homo sapiens didn't—

ALAN: OK, I get—

SYBIL: And Columbus didn't hit a sandbar somewhere and sink and drown, and our ancestors were lucky enough to survive through the plague and Hitler lost and here we are having dinner in safety and we're happy.

ALAN: So…?

SYBIL: So what are the chances?

ALAN: Oh *those* chances. 1 in 976 billion. Roughly.

SYBIL: See? That's a rare kind of love.

Beat.

ALAN: But if things had gone another way, if events had branched in a different direction at any point in the past, somebody else could be sitting here, equally happy, talking about the same things. Maybe they'd be neanderthals. Maybe they'd be Nazi Neanderthals.

She playfully throws a napkin at him.

Seriously. Think of all the events that *weren't* and the people who aren't.

SYBIL: I know. And yet we are.

ALAN: Well. Lucky us.

SYBIL: Lucky me.

ALAN: And lucky me.

SYBIL: And lucky *me*.

ALAN: And lucky us.

They reach for each other with their hands. Lightning flash and thunder clap taking us to black and transition.

Scene 2

Projection: LOUIS and ANNA's home

LOUIS comes home, having had a few drinks. The room has the black silhouette in profile of a television. The title fades.

LOUIS: Hello Anna! *(Calling upstairs.)* Anna!?

He takes off his coat and throws it onto a chair. He pulss out the TV remote, sits, and turns the TV on. We hear the sounds of TV. He flips. He finds a soccer game on a French station.

ANNA comes in behind the TV, drying a pot.

(Feigning delight.) You're here.

ANNA: *(Icy.)* I am.

LOUIS: *(Redoubles the charm.)* I called your name.

ANNA continues to dry the pot.

ANNA: Are you hungry?

LOUIS: Not yet.

ANNA: Not yet?

LOUIS: In a little moment.

ANNA: It's eleven o'clock.

LOUIS: You know, in France, we eat very late.

ANNA: Yeah, well, we're not in France.

LOUIS: I had a crêpe.

ANNA: A crêpe? Where the hell did you eat a crêpe?

LOUIS: There is a new crêperie / just off of—

ANNA: So you're not hungry?

LOUIS: The crêpes were shit.

ANNA: So you're not hungry.

LOUIS: Maybe I will take a little bit of dinner in a moment.

ANNA: Are you drunk again?

LOUIS: Are you angry again?

Beat.

ANNA: So where were you? I tried calling you.

LOUIS: I was out with some of my students.

ANNA: Out with the kids!

LOUIS: They were *graduate* students, Anna.

ANNA: Who was it?

LOUIS: Rachel, and—

ANNA: Rachel—?

LOUIS: Yes *Rachel*, Anna. And Max, and Francis, and Sharon, and Bill.

ANNA: I thought we said you weren't going to see Rachel outside of class.

LOUIS: Look, it was a group evening. After the seminar. I can't avoid it if she is part of the group.

ANNA: You said you weren't—

LOUIS: Anna, it is *you* who said. For me it's not a big deal.

ANNA: You said you wanted to sleep with her.

LOUIS: I said I wanted to sleep with her AND you. It's not the same. And anyway, it's a fantaisie. *You're* the one who asked me about a fantaisie.

ANNA: Yes, but I wasn't asking which one of your students you'd like to—

LOUIS: Anna!

LOUIS turns off the TV. As sincere and conciliatory as possible.

It's nothing. It's…

I love you.

No response.

I said that I love you.

ANNA: I know.

ANNA leaves.

LOUIS: I see that you are not happy! I'm sorry!

As LOUIS begins to talk, more or less to himself, the television starts to fade out and a large circle of light fades in. It recalls both a dramatic spotlight and the moon.

I don't know why I do this. It is a torture for you and it is a torture for me. You are alone. But did you know that I am *always* alone. It's the first time I feel not alone in my life since my mother died. Since I was a *boy*. You make me so happy, Anna.

ANNA re-enters, sans pot. LOUIS turns to her, and as he snaps out of his reverie, the moon snaps out and the television snaps back in.

I will just watch a few more minutes, then I will have some dinner, and then I will come upstairs.

ANNA: Oh sorry, I just put your dinner out in the backyard for the dog.

Beat.

LOUIS: OK, well then I will watch a few more minutes and then I will go and see the dog and maybe he will let me share my dinner and *then* I will come to bed.

Pause.

ANNA: You drink too much.

LOUIS: Anna, come on. I have a glass of wine with my students, I come home. I want to watching the football and eat a bit of food and you give my dinner to the fucking dog? I say I love you and you don't say anything? Not everything is a drama. This is not your book.

ANNA: You haven't even read my book.

LOUIS: I told you, I will read it when you are finished.

ANNA: And don't start about my book. It takes a long time to write a book.

LOUIS: I know.

ANNA: Oh yeah here it goes!

She storms off stage and begins throwing books at LOUIS, which he attempts to dodge, during the following:

Just say it. You're better than me because you're published!

LOUIS: Anna—

ANNA: I mean who reads your books? Professors? Sycophantic graduate students? What, maybe a dozen people? And why? Professional obligation? Professional boredom?

A whole stack of magazines is thrown at LOUIS.

LOUIS: Stop!

He begins to clean up the mess she is making. ANNA re-enters, holding one of LOUIS' books.

ANNA: I mean *(Reading the title.)* "Quantitative Moral Systems and the Nature of Persons." What does that even MEAN?! (*Throws book at him which he ducks.)*

LOUIS: Anna!!

ANNA: Why is that important?

LOUIS: Because other people think it's important.

LOUIS exits to put the books and magazines away.

(Calling from off.) Because other people think it's important.

Beat.

ANNA: And so what I'm doing *isn't* important?

LOUIS: *(Re-entering.)* Well, I guess we will see.

Pause.

ANNA: I think you should leave.

Beat.

LOUIS: *(Laughing.)* What?

ANNA: I'd like you to leave.

LOUIS: What are you talking about?

ANNA: I think it's time that you go.

LOUIS: What do you mean?

ANNA: What do you mean, what do I mean? I want you to leave the house.

LOUIS: What the fuck are you talking about?

ANNA: Don't swear in my house.

LOUIS: In *your* house? Anna, I put in the down payment. I pay most of the mortgage while you write your fucking book.

ANNA: Get out.

LOUIS: Calm down Anna.

ANNA: Calm down Anna.

LOUIS: Anna, we can talk about this.

ANNA: There's nothing to talk about.

LOUIS: I'm not having a fucking AFFAIR!

ANNA: *(Silence.)*

LOUIS: OK?

ANNA: *(Silence.)*

LOUIS sits, turns on the TV.

LOUIS: I will sleep in the guest room.

ANNA: I want you to get out.

LOUIS: Anna, you can't just throw me out. I have nowhere to go.

ANNA: Get a hotel room.

LOUIS: You are throwing me out because of this story you have invented. You are—

ANNA: *(Suddenly screaming like a seven-year-old.)* Get out of my house I don't want this anymore I don't WANT this anymore I DON'T WANT WANT THIS ANYMORE GET OUT!!

Pause.

LOUIS: My God. What is what is going on inside you?

LOUIS looks at her in for a beat, then turns off TV, gathers his coat, looks back at ANNA.

Je sais pas ce qui se passe dans ta / tête

ANNA: Idon'tunderstandanythingyou'resaying!

LOUIS looks at her in disbelief, then leaves. As the scene dissolves…

Projection: Louis has been having an affair with Rachel for 7.5 weeks.

Lights fade out on ANNA trying to adhere to her resolve. Transition to:

Scene 3

A phone ringing. Lights up on ALAN at work, exercising. A silhouette of a desk with a computer.

He wears an earpiece, allowing him to continue to exercise while watching his monitor and carrying on the following conversation.

ALAN: *(Answering the phone.)* Yeah. Hi…Yeah, I'm looking at it now for the Balanced Power Annuity fund.

Well, it looks like a bargain, but I feel like it might go a little lower, I 'm just going to watch the action, I might wait as low as fifteen dollars… *(Looking at the screen.)* Fifteen twenty-five right now but it was over sixteen bucks this morning so…

He is grunting in the rhythm of his exercise.

What? No, unfortunately I'm just exercising… Yeah it was this weekend… 357th out of nearly two thousand people… Personal best, two hours twenty eight… Yes, significantly better than average, thank you.

He sees something on his computer screen.

See, there it is. Fifteen even. What'd I tell you?

He types in two numbers and clicks enter and then resumes his exercises.

Well, I guess we'll see how that plays out… It's not boring… Yes, but you see you have to *invite* the pain… Oh, I don't know. I do things to occupy my mind. Like, I count my steps, right, and every time I— …No, just in my head… Well, I do them in fives, I don't even think about it… For the whole race? I don't know, around thirty-eight and a half thousand, anyway, let me finish. So everytime I pass a fire hydrant I take the number of steps that I've run and I try to figure out of its factors before I pass the next one… Yes, almost exactly like *Rain Man*…

Well, the next one's in a month, but we'll have a two-week-old and also I'm scheduled to have an operation—

Nah, it's not a big deal.

Something said on the other side of the conversation causes him to look at his screen. Beat.

Yeah I see it… Very weird.

Now. Oh shit!! Uh, listen, I'll call you back.

He hangs up. A look of shock on his face.

That was a lot of money.

Blackout and transition to:

Scene 4

ANNA sits cross-legged. She has a white laptop beside her. SYBIL sits next to her.

SYBIL: So, what do I do?

ANNA, distracted, fiddles with the touchpad on her laptop, choosing a song from her music player software.

ANNA: Ummm, well, you just sit in the lotus or half lotus or just like this if you can't.

SYBIL: Like this?

ANNA: Huh? just a second *(Adjusting something on her laptop, then glancing quickly over.)* …yup that's good it's really too bad that Alan isn't here a lot of the stuff I had planned is for couples.

SYBIL: It's OK.

ANNA: It's just I actually really wanted to use this as a practice teaching session—

SYBIL: It's hard for him to get away from work.

ANNA: Because I think there's a need for this in this community. Because people are always pregnant, right? And maybe if I developed a workshop, I could probably teach it like four or even six times a year.

SYBIL: You probably could.

ANNA: Did I tell you I'm thinking about opening my own studio?

SYBIL: When did you decide that?

ANNA: I haven't decided I just think maybe I'd be good at running a business do you think you'd come?

SYBIL: Well, I don't really do yoga.

ANNA: No but I mean if I had a studio.

SYBIL: *(Microbeat.)* I might.

Pause.

ANNA: Do you think I'm flaky?

Beat.

SYBIL: Why?

ANNA: I don't know. Sometimes my instincts tell me I'm so right about something, and then I end up changing my mind I don't think I'm a very good writer.

SYBIL: You're a great write/r.

ANNA: You've never read anything of mine. *(Beat.)* We should start should we start?

Beat.

SYBIL: What's important is that you do something you love.

SYBIL's phone rings or buzzes.

Sorry, it's Alan. I'll just put it on silent.

ANNA: Technology.

ANNA presses the spacebar on her computer, beginning the soothing track that she's been cueing up. She guides SYBIL through a meditation.

I want you to close your eyes. And go to the centre of your breath. And *breathe.*

ANNA takes a deep breath and SYBIL follows along.

Turn your awareness inside and find stillness and peace. And *Silence.*

Another breath.

Quiet your mind.

Take the opportunity to *rest* yourself from external distractions and *experience* the silence that is available to you now and in every moment.

Pause.

Silence is not something we normally allow ourselves to experience in our daily lives and why is it that we are unable to do just that?

A smile is on SYBIL's face. A breath. As ANNA continues, SYBIL's eyes open and she looks at ANNA, who still has her eyes closed.

Allow your mind to feel tranquil, peaceful, and serene. And *Silent.*

A breath. SYBIL decides that ANNA is finally finished talking and closes her eyes. As ANNA starts talking again, SYBIL tries very hard to hold in her laughter.

Why is it that we always feel we need to fill the air with words and words when silence would suffice?

SYBIL is now shaking trying to contain her laughter while maintaining her meditation pose.

Now allow yourself to fully relax into this space of stillness, to find this inner silence.

Experience this peace and serenity.

ANNA is fighting waves of anxiety and tears.

Experience it.

ANNA's crying becomes more evident, catching SYBIL's attention.

Experience it.

SYBIL: Anna?

ANNA: And try to hold onto it. Try your best.

ANNA tries to fight back the tears.

SYBIL: Anna, are you OK?

ANNA: Keep breathing.

ANNA gives into her tears. SYBIL comforts her.

SYBIL: Hey… It's OK… Here. Come here.

Fade to black and transition to:

Scene 5

Music. ALAN and LOUIS sit together. They are drinking scotch.

Projection: ALAN and LOUIS are at a bar

LOUIS: Do you want to know the meaning of life Alan?

Projection: They are both drunk

ALAN: 42?

Projection: They do this every week

LOUIS: No, Alan, it is not 42. You want me to explain it to you? Well OK.

To start we have to define the terms. First: "Life". What does "life" *mean*? Well, it's the opposite of death, no? You are either alive or you are dead. So someone can say, "I feel so alive" but it doesn't mean fucking anything. You are alive or you are not alive. These are the two choices. Like in a computer. One is a yes, Zero is a no. One, zero. On, off. Go, Stop. Life, death. OK? So "life" is "one."

So OK, now we have: "what's the *meaning* of *one*?"

So next: "meaning". "Meaning" is *significance*. What significance does it have for us, and another way of saying significance is value. What value does it have?

So when you say "What's the *meaning* of *life*?" really, you are asking "What's the *value* of one?"

So it's just one. Not 42. *One*.

The loneliest number. We are alone, and we cannot depend on anybody else.

ALAN: Did you know that I lost thirteen million dollars of my company's money the other day?

Beat.

LOUIS: What?! That's a lot!

ALAN: You're telling me.

LOUIS: How did you do that?

ALAN: Typo. I accidentally paid fifteen-one dollars for fifteen dollar shares. Three hundred and fifty thousand of them.

Beat as LOUIS tries to decipher ALAN's cavalier attitude.

LOUIS: You can *do* that?

ALAN: You can.

Beat.

LOUIS: Putain! Did they… Will they fire you?

ALAN: Almost certainly.

LOUIS: I'm sorry Alan.

ALAN: Ah well, you know. There are people in India who salvage plastic bags from garbage dumps for a living. I'll be alright. Little accidents happen all the time. *(Beat.)* And I'm getting one of my testicles removed.

LOUIS, who has just had a sip of scotch, does a spit-take.

LOUIS: What!?

ALAN: Yeah, I found out a couple of weeks ago.

LOUIS: Alan, that is not good.

ALAN: Actually it's not too bad. Survival rate is 98%. And I'm only stage one. So…

LOUIS: Which testicle?

ALAN: The left.

LOUIS takes a sharp intake of breath and shakes his head.

LOUIS: Do you know the story of Job, Alan?

ALAN: Like from the Bible, Job? Vaguely…

LOUIS: The man who had everything taken away by God as a way of testing his faith.

ALAN: Yes?

LOUIS: What do you think of this story?

ALAN: Well… I don't know. It's… I mean. I don't know. What do you think?

LOUIS: I think it is a shitty story.

Beat. LOUIS smirks.

ALAN: I have faith in two things: *Averages* and *randomness.* Which serves to remind me that I, by any standard, enjoy an above average existence. And it also offers me a great deal of comfort when shit happens.

LOUIS: Still, you're very unlucky.

ALAN: Luck is just probability taken personally. Do you enjoy teaching?

LOUIS: I don't like institutions.

Beat.

ALAN: You should try to work it out with my sister. Married men live about two and a half years longer. And your insurance premiums will be lower.

Beat.

Where are you staying?

LOUIS: On a park bench.

Beat.

ALAN: Really?

LOUIS: No, not "*Really.*" A toast: to your ball.

Transition to:

Scene 6

SYBIL alone onstage.

Projection: SYBIL

(Add the words "This is" to complete the phrase:)

This is SYBIL

SYBIL: OK everybody, it's time to stop colouring. Benjamin, can you put down your crayon?

Projection: She holds a masters degree in criminology

Thank you. Addison I see what you're doing.

Projection: She finds this training very useful

In a moment you can ask Timothy if he'd like to share, but now just listen. So, you all know that my baby is getting bigger in my belly. Well, sometime in the next few days, it's going to be time for the baby to come out. And so this is going to be my last day here in class. *(Answering a question.)* No, I won't be back on Monday, or the Monday after. No I won't be back to teach you at all this year, but maybe after I have my baby I can come back to see you. I'll miss all of you too. Yes, why doesn't everybody come up for one last touch of my belly.

Projection: SYBIL has been trying for four years to get pregnant

Transition to:

Scene 7

ALAN and ANNA in a café.

ANNA: Thirteen million dollars?

ALAN: Before we get there, what are you wearing?

ANNA: Clothes.

ALAN: No, on your head.

ANNA: It's a bindi.

ALAN: A bindi?

ANNA: Yeah.

ALAN: Are you Hindu all of a sudden?

ANNA: No.

ALAN: So why are you wearing it?

ANNA: Because I want to.

ALAN: Why?

ANNA: I think it looks nice.

He looks at her for a moment, shakes his head.

ALAN: I'm getting a coffee do you want a coffee?

ANNA: Soy latte.

ALAN: Really? Anna, that stuff is full of estrogen, it's not good for you.

ANNA: We weren't designed to drink cow's milk.

ALAN: Do you think that soy milk is naturally occurring? You know, ever since you started doing yoga—

ANNA: It has nothing to do with yoga.

ALAN: It does actually. It's all part of this new… It's like when you decided you wanted to be a nun.

ANNA: It is n—

ALAN: It's exactly the same thing.

ANNA: That was a long time ago.

ALAN: So what? It's the same impulse.

ANNA: What impulse?

ALAN: Avoidance.

ANNA: No.

ALAN: Escape.

ANNA: No!

ALAN: Well what then? Mom dies and you decide you want to be a nun. Your marriage starts falling apart and you start drinking soy everything and decide you're a Hindu or a Wiccan or a yogi or whatever it is?

ANNA: Wow. A little angry.

ALAN: I'm not angry.

ANNA: How can one person lose that much money?

ALAN: Oh, look, little mistakes happen in every kind of job. It's just sometimes little mistakes cost 13 million dollars.

Beat.

ANNA: My marriage isn't falling apart.

ALAN: No?

ANNA: And anyway, who are you to say anything about other peoples' belief systems? Who are you, here, now, who has grown up with such a narrow perspective of life—

ALAN: It's not narrow.

ANNA: It's like looking through-a-keyhole-from-50-frickin-paces narrow.

ALAN: Actually no, what I'm saying, is why are you, from the same perspective, why do you feel like all of a sudden the answers are in the fucking *orient*? I mean yes, I'm not into religion or mystical pursuits or whatever, but if you need a delusion, why not pick a home grown variety?

ANNA: Maybe I like it.

ALAN: Yeah, but it's a bit trendy. I mean what's wrong with Catholicism?

ANNA: Alan—

ALAN: It could be so retro. You might start a fad.

ANNA: It's not a trend. It's about giving your life a sense of meaning.

ALAN: *Meaning*. What does that *mean*?

ANNA: You don't believe our lives have meaning?

ALAN: To who?

ANNA: You don't think it means anything that we're here right now, having this conversation?

ALAN: Means what it means to you. Means what it means to me.

ANNA: You don't think it's changing, even in some minute way, our destinies?

ALAN: *Destiny*? What is this, Ancient Greece? OK, let's say tomorrow we find out the soy milk that they have here is contaminated because of an e. coli outbreak at the factory and there's a massive product recall and everybody who has drank from this particular batch has died tragically and in fact, not having soy has *saved your life*. Does that give my sage advice that you shouldn't drink soy milk any more *meaning*?

ANNA: Alan—

ALAN: Of course it doesn't, it just makes for a happy coincidence.

ANNA: You talk a lot, you know that?

ALAN: Listen, I'm just getting going. I mean, it seems to me that if you're looking for meaning in life, you're just setting yourself up for disappointment. Like that completely stupid question, why do bad things happen to good people? Well actually, bad things happen to good people because they're subject to the same mathematical probability as anybody else. Like me: Why do I have testicular cancer. Why am I probably going to lose my job? Now I can dress that up, and call it fate, and I can scream "Why me?" and pretend that there is some person or God or force to ask the question to. On the other hand why do good things happen? Like: Why am I a math genius? Why was I born so devastatingly handsome? There's no point worrying about it. There's no cosmic moral balancing out happening. There's just the things that happen to us and there's the stories we tell ourselves about whether we *deserve* them or not.

ANNA: You done?

ALAN: I'm just saying I think you've latched onto this new fascination in eastern mysticism to avoid dealing with certain realities. Instead of admitting to yourself that maybe you're not capable of making your marriage work, you're hiding behind all of this bindi-wearing, karma-slinging, downward doggism.

ANNA: Downward doggism?

ALAN: Yep.

ANNA: Did you just make that up?

ALAN: Divine inspiration.

Beat.

ANNA: Yeah, well, I think you're compiling Karma.

ALAN: So we can agree to disagree.

ANNA: Mmmm. (*Beat.*) I can't imagine why we don't hang out more often.

ALAN: Yeah I know. It's *refreshing* isn't it.

ANNA: I'm incapable of making a marriage work?

ALAN: Anna, you're on, you're off. A marriage isn't a light-switch.

Beat.

ANNA: Do you think…?

ALAN: What?

ANNA: I don't know… Nothing. (*Beat.*) How's Sybil?

Projection: SYBIL will give birth in 192 hours

ALAN: She's coming along.

ANNA: Do you guys need anything?

ALAN: No, I think we're doing OK.

ANNA: OK, well let me know.

Projection: The baby will die in its third day of life

Fade to black. Transition to:

Act II

Scene 1

LOUIS enters looking like a hobo and carrying a sleeping bag. He looks at the audience, sits on a chair, and pulls the sleeping bag over himself. Around him forms the silhouette of a park bench and a tree. ANNA enters. At first she doesn't recognize him.

ANNA: Louis?

LOUIS: Anna.

ANNA: What are you doing?

LOUIS: Je suis assis sur un banc dans le parc.

Beat.

ANNA: What?

LOUIS: Je suis assis sur un banc dans le / parc.

ANNA: Why are you speaking French?

LOUIS: Pourquoi? Pourquoi est-ce que tu m'as chassé de ma propre maison? / Pourquoi est-ce que tu as si peu confiance en moi que tu m'as jete à la rue comme un chien? Tu n'as aucune preuve qu'il s'est passé quoi que ce soit entre Rachel et moi, ni personne. Et en plus, elle m'a quitté. On s'voit plus.

ANNA: What is this some kind of screwed up power thing? You want to exclude me? You want to point up the fact that I'm stupid because I only speak one language? Well, no Louis, shut up! I don't care if you are smarter than me. I'm comfortable with myself, OK?! Are you drunk?

LOUIS: Et alors, quoi? Ça te dérange si je bois? Pourquoi est-ce que ça te dérange, toi ma femme? Mon ex-femme. Tout à coup tu t'inquiètes pour moi? Bon, va-t'en! Tu'veux plus de moi. J'ai plus besoin de toi. Casse toi. Je m'en fous.

ANNA: You are! You're drunk aren't you? It's seven o'clock in the morning. I'm leaving. You're a mess. LOUIS YOU'RE ACTING CRAZY!

Beat.

Projection: LOUIS has finished.

The university called. They said you stopped going to class. Your students are calling the house, they want their papers back. What is going on?

LOUIS: Rien.

ANNA: *(ANNA swallows down her frustration.)* Are you sleeping here? Across from the house?! Wait a second, are you stalking me? You're stalking me aren't you?! You can't just stalk someone Louis. Do you know how fucked up that is to stalk your own wife? Well you can't have this bench, go find some other bench. When I kicked you out I meant go further.

LOUIS: Fous moi la paix.

ANNA: Louis!!

She tries to think of something to say, but can't, and leaves.

Scene 2

The scene dissolves around LOUIS. He looks out at the audience, throws aside his sleeping bag. A vertical blue stripe is projected onto him.

Projection: LOUIS in blue

A red stripe is added on the opposite side of the stage. Then a white stripe between them, forming a French flag. A simultaneous English translation of LOUIS' speech, scrolling upwards, appears in the white stripe. He speaks directly to the audience.

LOUIS: Quand nous nous sommes separés,

Projection: When we seperated,

Je me suis dit, bon: Louis, ça y est.

Projection: I said to myself, alright Louis, go ahead.

Tu es libre. Enfin.

Projection: You're free. Finally.

T'as vécu ta vie de marié, T'as fait de ton mieux.

Projection: You've lived your married life, you did your best.

Et alors maintenant.

Projection: So what now?

La vie est devant toi.

Projection: Life is ahead of you.

Toutes les portes sont ouvertes.

Projection: All the doors are open.

Tu peux faire ce que tu veux.

Projection: You can do whatever you want.

Et alors je me suis dit: explorons…

Projection: So I thought to myself, why not explore

L'HÉDONISME.

Projection: HEDONISM

Et pendant les quinze jours suivants, je me suis soûlé quand j'en avais envie,

Projection: And for the next fortnight, I got drunk whenever I wanted to

c'est à dire tous les jours, tout le temps.

Projection: which was all day, every day.

J'ai quitté mon boulot

Projection: I left my job

ou plutot, j'ai arrêté d'y aller,

Projection: or, rather, stopped going.

j'ai depensé tout mon fric

Projection: I spent all my savings

Et j'ai vécu dans la rue.

Projection: and I lived on the street.

The roll of thunder. It begins to rain on LOUIS.

J'ai couché avec plusieurs femmes.

Projection: I slept with many women

Enfin, deux.

Projection: Well, two.

À chacune je n'ai parlé qu'en français.

Projection: And I only spoke in French to them.

Elles ne pouvaient pas me comprendre.

Projection: They couldn't understand me.

Par contre, moi…j'ai tout compris.

Projection: But I understood everything.

Et les soirs où je n'arrivais pas à séduire de gonzesses,

Projection: And the nights where I couldn't seduce a woman

Je dormais dans la rue,

Projection: I slept on the street,

sur un banc, dans le parc.

Projection: on a park bench.

Après quelques nuits dehors,

Projection: After a few nights outside

je puais tellement que je n'attirais plus personne,

Projection: I smelled so bad that I couldn't seduce anybody

même pas une pute.

Projection: not even a whore.

Et de toute façon les putes ne m'interessais pas.

Projection: But I wasn't interested in whores anyway.

C'est comme ça que j'ai passé deux semaines entirès,

Projection: And that's how I spent the whole two weeks.

comme un chien dans la rue.

Projection: Like a dog on the streets.

Seul avec ma tristesse.

Projection: Alone in my sadness.

LOUIS' head circle lifts off, floats up, becoming the moon. A dog howls at the moon.

Transition to:

Scene 3

ANNA sits cross-legged, meditating. Sounds of nature. The following words are projected beside her.

Projection: Shhhh

Beat.

Anna is on a week-long silent meditation retreat

Pause.

She is trying to clear her mind

Sound of a fly.

ANNA swats at it.

She hasn't had sex in 87 days

Beat.

And frankly, it's getting to be a little much.

Pause.

She's thinking about having sex with the guru

Beat.

In the woods behind the temple

A tiny smile on ANNA's face.

Ohhhh yeah…

Music. Transition to:

Scene 4

ALAN and SYBIL at the dinner table. SYBIL is in a bathrobe. She's an utterly different person than the one we met prviously. She stares absently into space.

ALAN: Your silence isn't making any of this easier.

SYBIL: *(Silence.)*

ALAN: I tried calling Anna again.

SYBIL: *(Silence.)*

ALAN: My day was fine. Same old same old.

SYBIL: *(Silence.)*

ALAN: Actually, I called in to work. Apparently they haven't decided whether or not to fire me yet. I think now they're waiting.

SYBIL: *(Silence.)*

ALAN: You know, I've heard that over 50% of marriages end up in divorce after losing a child, but I looked it up and it turns out it's only 12%.

SYBIL: Why are you doing this to me?

ALAN: Doing what?

SYBIL: Doing what.

ALAN: Doing what.

SYBIL: *(Silence.)*

ALAN: We can't... The thing is, Syb, it's so statistically improbable, but it does happen, and it's...it's just... you know it happens. It doesn't mean that you did anything wr—

SYBIL: Shut up. Please please please please please, I'm begging you Shut Up!

Silence.

ALAN looks helplessly at SYBIL, then pours himself a glass of wine. He puts down the bottle and looks at SYBIL. The glass explodes. The bottle explodes. The room explodes.

Blackout.

Scene 5

In the black we hear the sound of rain. The following titles are projected, one at a time.

Projection: It's raining

LOUIS stands outside ANNA's window

He's bored of living on the street

LOUIS appears.

He sings "Ne Me Quitte Pas" by Jacques Brel.

A karaoke version of "Ne Me Quitte Pas" begins. The projector translates.

LOUIS: Ne me quitte pas

Don't leave me

Il faut oublier

We must forget

Tout peut s'oublier

Everything can be forgotten

Qui s'enfuit déjà

It's already escaping

Oublier le temps

Forget the times

Des malentendus

Of misunderstandings

Et le temps perdu

And the lost time

À savoir comment

To know how

Oublier ces heures

To forget the hours

Qui tuaient parfois

Which sometimes killed

À coups de pourquoi

With blows of "why?"

Le coeur du bonheur

The heart of happiness

Ne me quitte pas

Don't leave me

Ne me quitte pas

Don't leave me

Ne me quitte pas

Don't leave me

Ne me quitte pas

Don't leave me

The following and the other projected commentaries during the song are projected on a different area than the lyrics.

This song runs four mins and 11 seconds

Moi je t'offrirai

Me, I will offer you

Des perles de pluie

Pearls of rain

Venues de pays

From countries

Oú il ne pleut pas

Where it never rains

Je creus'rai la terre

I will dig the ground

Jusqu'après ma mort

Until after my death

Pour couvrir ton corps

To cover your body

D'or et de lumiêre;

With gold and light

Je f'rai un domaine

I will create a kingdom

Où l'amour s 'ra roi

Where love will be king

Où l'amour s'ra loi

Where love will be law

Où tu seras reine

And you will be queen

Ne me quitte pas

Don't leave me

Ne me quitte pas

Don't leave me

LOUIS sang in the church choir as a boy.

Ne me quitte pas

Don't leave me

Ne me quitte pas

Don't leave me

He loved wearing the robes.

Ne me quitte pas

Don't leave me

Je t'inventerai

For you, I will invent

Des mots insensés

Senseless words

Que tu comprendras

That you will understand

Je te parlerai

I will speak to you

De ces amants là

Of those lovers

Qui ont vu deux fois

Who have twice seen

Leurs coeurs s'embraser

Their hearts catch fire

Je te racont'rai

I will tell you

L'histoire de ce roi

The story of a King

Mort de n'avoir pas pu te rencontrer

Who died from never having met you

Ne me quitte pas

Don't leave me

Ne me quitte pas

Don't leave me

Ne me quitte pas

Don't leave me

This is exactly the half-way point in the song

Ne me quitte pas

Don't leave me

Ne me quitte pas

Don't leave me

On a vu souvent

Oftentimes we've seen

Rejaillir le feu

The fire reignite

De l'ancien volcan

In an ancient volcano

Qu'on croyait trop vieux

Once thought too old

Il est paraît-il

It would seem

Des terres brûlées

That scorched earth

Donnant plus de blé

Gives more wheat

Qu'un meilleur avril

Than the best of Aprils

Et quand vient le soir

And when the evening comes,

Pour qu'un ciel flamboie

To enflame the night sky

Le rouge et le noir

Musn't red and black

Ne s'épousent-ils pas

Must get married, no?

Ne me quitte pas

Don't leave me

Ne me quitte pas

Don't leave me

Ne me quitte pas

Don't leave me

Ne me—

Don't...

(Spoken.) Je suis un cliché.

(I'm a cliché.

Je suis un désastre

I'm a disaster.)

Ne me quitte pas

Don't leave me

Je ne vais plus pleurer

I won't cry anymore

Je ne vais plus parler

I won't speak anymore

Je me cacherai là

I will hide myself

À te regarder

To watch you

Danser et sourire

Dancing and smiling

Et à t'écouter

And listen to you

Chanter et puis rire

Singing and laughing

Laisse-moi devenir

Let me become

A stage direction fades in very slowly as the song continues.

Projection: Stage direction: ANNA appears at her window, looking down at LOUIS. She watches him. He looks up to see her.

L'ombre de ton ombre

The shadow of your shadow

L'ombre de ta main

The shadow of your hand

L'ombre de ton chien

The shadow of your dog

Mais ne me quitte pas

But don't leave me

Ne me quitte pas!

Don't leave me!

Ne me quitte pas!!

Don't leave me!!

NE ME—!!!

DON'T!!!

LOUIS' song is interrupted by a loud crash of thunder.

ANNA: *(Off, yelling.)* What the hell are you doing Louis? Frig off!

The music cuts out, LOUIS stops singing. leaving nothing except the sound of the rain.

LOUIS: Mais…

But…

Blackout and transition to:

Scene 6

Sound of a phone ringing. SYBIL enters. She is seen in one of two rectangles projected with rain to suggest windows in her house. She holds a wireless phone. She presses the button to answer but just looks at the phone for a time. As she eventually brings the receiver up to her ear, we hear ANNA's voice on the phone.

ANNA: Sybil?… Are you there? …Alan told me that you'd stopped talking.

I'm so sorry.

SYBIL pulls the phone away and the volume of ANNA's voice drops.

If there's anything I can do…

Are you there? I can hear you breathing so I know you're there… It's OK. We can just talk like th—

SYBIL takes the batteries out of the phone. The doorbell rings. She turns to see LOUIS standing in her doorway, looking like a drowned rat, his clothes dirty and torn.

A beat while LOUIS each takes in the extent of her transformation.

LOUIS: Bonsoir Sybil.

Pause.

SYBIL: Louis?

LOUIS: C'est moi.

Pause.

SYBIL: You look terrible Louis.

LOUIS: Je suis un peu sale.

Pause.

SYBIL: Come in.

LOUIS enters. Silence. They look at each other.

LOUIS: Merci de me laisser entrer. Je sais que j'pu. Même aû Tim Hortons on ne me laisse plus utiliser les toilettes.

Beat.

Et toi Sybil? Ça va?

SYBIL: Oh, well…

LOUIS: La tristesse.

SYBIL: La tristesse? Oui Louis.

LOUIS: Je comprends.

Beat.

SYBIL: Louis… I try to think about things I might like to do. I think I should go back to school and study history, but I don't have the energy to even look at when the classes start, much less get myself registered.

I can barely get out of bed to go to the bathroom. I wouldn't even bother, except it would be more work to clean myself up.

And poor Alan… I hate him. Je le déteste Louis.

I want my baby.

They slowly begin to move towards each other and embrace. She cries on his shoulder. She suddenly and violently throws him off in shock and disblief.

You smell terrible!

LOUIS: Je—

SYBIL: Why do you smell so awful? Go upstairs right now! Go and take a shower!

LOUIS: Je préfère—

SYBIL: I don't care!! You need to start behaving normally! Go. Shave! Shower! Wash! You smell like feces. Pull yourself together! Wash yourself. Bathe yourself. You're a grown-up. It's time. Do it! Go!

LOUIS: Sybil—

SYBIL: Louis, go upstairs and don't come back until you're clean!!

LOUIS exits. Music, rain, thunder building up over a sequence in which SYBIL tries to pull herself together, and we see LOUIS in the shower. As the music builds to a climax, they slowly turn towards each other.

Snap to:

Scene 7

LOUIS wearing a towel only. SYBIL is wearing bright red lipstick, which we have not seen her put on.

LOUIS: Sybil?

SYBIL: *(Quickly.)* Yes?

LOUIS: I have done it.

She looks at him, standing there is his towel, for a beat.

SYBIL: I put your clothes in the washing machine.

Beat.

You look much better.

LOUIS: I feel better.

SYBIL: I'm not surprised. You looked almost inhuman.

LOUIS: I was on the street for two weeks.

SYBIL: *(Beat.)* Why? Were you depressed?

LOUIS: Not…no.

SYBIL: No?

LOUIS: It was a kind of experiment.

SYBIL: *(Beat.)* And?

LOUIS: And what?

SYBIL: What were the results of your "experiment"?

LOUIS: I was lonely.

Pause. They stare at each other.

SYBIL: *(Breaking his gaze.)* Do you want a cup of tea?

LOUIS: OK.

SYBIL: Do you take anything in it?

LOUIS: A lot of sugar and milk.

SYBIL: A lot of sugar?

LOUIS: Yes.

SYBIL: How much?

LOUIS: A lot.

SYBIL: How much is a lot?

LOUIS: Just put in whatever is a lot for you and then add another spoonful.

Beat.

SYBIL: That's disgusting Louis.

LOUIS: Yes, I know but I don't care. Well, I do care, but I also…don't.

In one sudden motion, he drops his towel.

SYBIL: Louis what are you doing?

Pause.

What are you doing?

He doesn't respond. He merely stands there, naked, looking at her in the eyes. Suddenly sh runs as hard at him as she can, smashing her body him, and wraps her arms around him, embracing him hard. He embraces her.

ALAN enters. At first, they don't see him.

ALAN: Oh.

LOUIS and SYBIL snap out of their embrace and look at ALAN, caught.

OK.

ALAN leaves.

Blackout and transition to:

Act III

Scene 1

ALAN and SYBIL in bed, in birds-eye-view. Heavy rain can be seen through the window beside their bed. The sound of a ticking clock.

ALAN: *(Mild as hell.)* I guess I'm a little bit surprised.

SYBIL: *(Silence.)*

ALAN: Do you hear me you do hear me, right?

SYBIL: *(Silence.)*

ALAN: Because I'm talking and I want to make sure that what you're doing is in fact conscious. That you're not just shutting me out...inadvertently or something.

SYBIL: *(Silence.)*

ALAN: I mean, you're not deaf. I know you're not deaf.

SYBIL: I hear you Louis.

He shoots a look at her. Beat.

I mean Alan.

ALAN: Oh good. *(Beat.)* Why?

SYBIL: I don't know.

ALAN: But really, though, why?

SYBIL: *(She thinks.)*

ALAN: Well?

SYBIL: I guess I don't know.

ALAN: I think you do.

SYBIL: What do you think Alan? That I'm having an affair?

ALAN: I'm sorry. What am I supposed to think?

SYBIL: *(Silence.)*

ALAN: That's just fucking terrific.

SYBIL: *(Flatly.)* I'm not.

ALAN: Deny it a little more forcefully Syb.

SYBIL: I'm not fighting with you.

ALAN: Well, I *am*!

SYBIL: *(Silence.)*

ALAN: And more silence.

SYBIL: Please—

ALAN: Don't tell me to shut up. Don't tell me to "please shut up." Don't beg me. Don't assume that I'm going to just give up and be happy living with a walking corpse for the rest of my life. I'm not. You're taking away my right to fight for us.

SYBIL: *(Silence.)*

ALAN: *(Very suddenly.)* FUCK!

SYBIL: I'm going to sleep in the baby's room.

Music and rain. Projection of rain as the stage clears.

V.O.: Later this evening, in her sleep, Sybil will be struck by lightning, hospitalised, and rendered comatose.

The odds of this happening in a person's lifetime are 6250 to 1.The odds of surviving a lighting strike are greater than of dying from a lightning strike.

Did you know that?

Sound of thunder.

Of course Alan will be devastated.

But he will be as devastated by his ambivalence as he is by his loss.

Isn't that interesting?

Thunderclap, taking us into:

Scene 2

SYBIL lies on a stretcher. ALAN and ANNA stare at her, in shock.

ANNA: It's too weird. I mean, it's really really… Why is all this stuff happening to you?

ALAN: I don't really wanna talk about it.

Beat.

How was the silent retreat?

ANNA: Oh you know. Pretty quiet. (*Pause.*) Sorry. That was supposed to be—

ALAN: I got it.

ANNA: I'm sorry, I know it's not the time to joke you must be so/worried.

ALAN: It's fine. It helps to talk about something else.

ANNA: I'm sorry. (*Pause.*) I feel renewed.

ALAN: Good.

ANNA: Like a new person.

ALAN: That's great.

ANNA: It was transcendent.

ALAN: I'm glad you found it useful.

Pause.

ANNA: To tell you the truth?

ALAN: Um hm?

ANNA: It's very difficult.

ALAN: I see.

ANNA: It's just a lot of time with yourself.

ALAN: Right.

ANNA: Which is hard.

ALAN: Well—

ANNA: I mean because we're awful, aren't we.

ALAN: I d

ANNA: People are really terribly broken. And to face that in yourself. To face up to what you're truly feeling when you're not pretending for anybody, not even yourself that's a pretty horrible scary place.

Beat.

ALAN: So you enjoyed it then.

ANNA: And I slept with the guru.

Long pause.

ALAN: That make any noise?

ANNA: I'm sorry. This is really not the right time—

ALAN: I think Sybil is having an affair with Louis.

Infidelity everywhere.

Pause. ANNA looks at SYBIL.

ANNA: Wow.

Beat. Blackout.

Scene 3

LOUIS in an alley standing next to an oil drum with a fire in it. ALAN enters. LOUIS is made visibly uncomfortable by ALAN's presence.

ALAN: Hi Louis.

LOUIS: Alan.

ALAN hands LOUIS a flask. LOUIS tentatively accepts it and drinks.

ALAN: So you're still out here, are you?

LOUIS: Oui.

Beat as ALAN swallows down the fact that LOUIS is still speaking French.

ALAN: You doing well?

LOUIS: Je ne peux pas me plaindre.

Et toi?

ALAN: What?!

LOUIS: Toi.

ALAN: You're asking how I am? I'm not too good, Louis.

LOUIS: Je comprends.

ALAN: "Je comprends." You understand? I'm quite certain that you don't. (*Beat.*) So what's with the French,

Louis?

Beat.

LOUIS: It's a nice language.

Beat.

ALAN: Right.

LOUIS: Do you want to hurt me?

ALAN: That would be the sensible thing to do, don't you think?

Beat.

LOUIS: How's Sybil?

ALAN: Not very well.

LOUIS: Is she awake?

ALAN: No.

Were you sleeping with her?

LOUIS: No, Alan.

ALAN: Really?

LOUIS: Really Alan.

ALAN: You know, I think I believe you?

Beat.

So life on the street, hey? My life is uh…pretty crazy just at the moment. As you maybe can imagine. Or not. Probably not actually. So I gotta tell you that when I see you choosing… Choosing misery. You know, choosing this horseshit about living on the… I mean, what the fuck is wrong with you? You had a fight. Make up. Work on it. I mean, really. How dare you not work it out. How dare you choose misery, when there's— You don't need to be living like this.

LOUIS: She kicked me out.

ALAN: So what? You have some control over the situation.

LOUIS: She insisted.

ALAN: And what did you do? You shut down communication. I mean, really, Louis, for the sake of the rest of us who have actual tragedy, work it the fuck out. Exert a little control. And you know, maybe you're not 100% happy with Anna. But who's 100% happy? She's good enough. And maybe she's not easy to live with but that doesn't mean that you have to go and ruin my— I mean if you hadn't…that's why she ended up in the guest room!

LOUIS: It's really not my fault, Alan.

Beat.

ALAN: Actually it *is*. (*Beat.*) I'm going back to the hospital. Do whatever you want.

ALAN exits. Blackout.

Scene 4

Projection: Stage direction: SYBIL is wheeled into frame on a gurney in the transition.

Dimly, we see this play out. The following text is added:

A pulsing line is projected on the wall, it is SYBIL's heart monitor.

The lights reveal ALAN standing over SYBIL, comatose on a gurney. A heart monitor line appears, pulsing, and we hear the beep of the machine.

ALAN: Hey Syb.

Listen, I talked to the doctors and uh... I asked them what they thought your chances are. Apparently they hate that question.

Anyway, I think you just gotta open your eyes. Alright? OK, come on now, OK? Just sit up and we can talk about all this, OK?

Please? Please open your eyes? Come on you FUCKING—!

He shakes the gurney but then immediately begins his apology.

I'm sorry I'm sorry I'm sorry. I'm just...

Come on, this has gone on for way too long now. OK? I'm getting worried.

In despair he kneels next to her, and whispers something into her ear.

Projection: *(This text appears as though being typed.)* After a few moments, SYBIL's eyes open, she looks at ALAN and smiles. ALAN lifts his head to see

A cursor, like ones in word processing programs begins to erase the second paragraph, stopping at the word "SYBIL's".

The following text is then added:

a ghost, perhaps a projected silhouette of her form, stands up, gets off the gurney, and exits.

A white silhouette of SYBIL's form sits up, and exits as we hear the monitor beep turn into a continuous tone and see the heart monitor line go flat.

ALAN: Syb? Sybil? No no no no somebody help us?! Sybil? No! Somebody help us! don't know what to do! I don't know what to do! I don't know what to do!

Sybil?! HELP! I don't know what to do!

As this line is projected a clap of thunder takes the stage to black.

Projection: The line goes flat.

Scene 5

There is a clock on the wall. The second hand spins. The room fades up. ALAN enters, he sits on a chair, staring into space. ANNA enters.

ANNA: How are you doing?

ALAN: I'm OK.

Pause.

ANNA: Do you feel like you're being tested?

ALAN: No. By who?

ANNA: The universe?

ALAN: For what purpose? (*Beat.*) How's your book going?

ANNA: I haven't written anything in a couple weeks. (*Beat.*) How are you?

ALAN: I told you, I'm OK, I just… I had no idea death was so expensive.

She puts her hand on his back to comfort him.

On the other hand insurance benefits go way up in cases of accidental death.

Beat.

Would you wish unhappiness on me?

ANNA: No.

ALAN: Because I'm bad, Anna. I mean, there's ways of

looking at me and saying, that man is bad—

ANNA: Alan.

ALAN: But there are worse. I mean if this *is* some kind of moral retribution—

ANNA: It's/not Alan

ALAN: Then it's really perverse because there are a lot of people who do really bad things, and this doesn't happen to them.

ANNA: Bad things happen.

ALAN: But not like this. I mean what is the probability that one person could…

Beat.

You want to know something funny? You know my operation? I got a call from my doctor. It turns out there was an error in my test results. They were looking at some other guy's chart. I don't need to go in for surgery after all. But the thing is I would literally give my left testicle to have my life back the way it was.

He tries to contain his tears.

ANNA: It's OK.

ALAN: To tell you the truth? It's kind of hard to feel anything other than despair right now.

ANNA: Well—

ALAN: I mean what else is there?

ANNA: There's—

ALAN: Seriuosly, what else is there. *(Pause.)* I thought you would have answers.

ANNA: Nothing that you'll find helpful.

She comforts him. LOUIS enters. ALAN lowers his head.

LOUIS: Sorry. How are you?

ALAN: I'm OK.

Beat.

LOUIS: *(To ANNA, quietly.)* Do we have detergent?

ANNA: There was some on top of the fridge.

LOUIS: Why was it on top of the fridge?

ANNA: I put it there.

Beat.

LOUIS exits. ALAN lifts his head.

ALAN: I have nothing!

ANNA: You have me.

ALAN: Yeah. Listen, I should…get home. I gotta— I'm not sure.

ANNA: You sure you don't want to stay?

ALAN: No, I uhhh… I should go.

ALAN leaves suddenly.

ANNA: *(Calling after him.)* Call me OK? If you need anything?

ALAN: *(From off.)* Sure.

ANNA: Alan?!

He is gone. ANNA, lost in thought, sits.

ANNA: *(Calling off.)* What time do you teach?

LOUIS: *(Off.)* Three.

ANNA: *(Calling off.)* I'm making meatballs

I'm going to do some writing.

I'm going to fold the laundry when it comes out of the dryer.

(To herself.) I'm going to read the whole Bible…

I'm going to start eating better…

I'm going to return the video that is three months overdue…

I'm going to exercise my kegels…

I'm going to flirt with strange men…

I'm going run away to South America while you're out…

(Utterly unconvinced.) I'm going to be better.

LOUIS: *(Re-entering.)* What?

ANNA: I'm making meatballs.

Beat.

LOUIS: Yum.

LOUIS exits leaving ANNA alone. The room fades to black except for the clock, which continues to mark time. A flashing cursor appears before the final words are typed:

Projection: The End

The cursor continues to blink after the text is typed. The clock fades. The words fade, leaving the stage in black

The End.